Piano White Pages

ISBN 1-4234-0468-8

CORPORATION

7777 W. BLUEMOUND RD. P.O. BOX 13819 MILWAUKEE, WI 53213

Visit Hal Leonard Online at
www.halleonard.com

Table of Contents

AFTER THE LOVE HAS GONE

Words and Music by DAVID FOSTER,
JAY GRAYDON and BILL CHAMPLIN

10

AFTER THE LOVIN'

Words and Music by ALAN BERNSTEIN
and RICHIE ADAMS

So, I sing you to sleep, __ af-ter __ the lov-in', with a
song I just wrote __ yes-ter-day. And I

13

I'm __ still in love _____ with you.

Mm, _

Af - ter the lov - in', _ I'm __ still in love with

you.

ALL NIGHT LONG
(All Night)

Words and Music by
LIONEL RICHIE

22

26

AMAZED

Words and Music by MARV GREEN,
CHRIS LINDSEY and AIMEE MAYO

Moderately slow Country Ballad

Ev -'ry time our eyes meet, this feel - in' in - side me
The smell_ of __ your skin, the taste_ of your kiss,

is al - most more _ than I _ can take. __
the way you whis - per in __ the dark. __

Recorded a half step lower.

28

AMANDA

Words and Music by
TOM SCHOLZ

34

ANGRY EYES

Words and Music by KENNY LOGGINS
and JIM MESSINA

43

blind - ness ___ binds ___ us to - geth - er in a

false dis - guise. _____ Can you ___ see ___

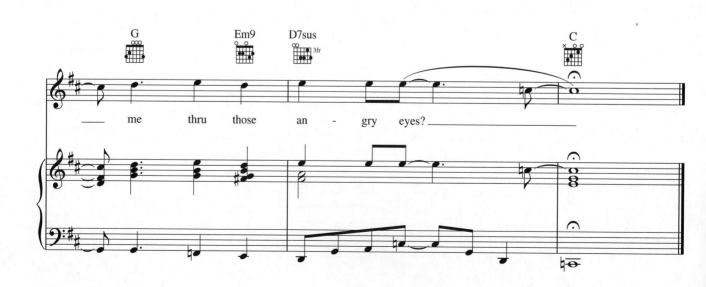

___ me thru those an - gry eyes? _____

BABY, I LOVE YOUR WAY

Words and Music by
PETER FRAMPTON

46

ANOTHER DAY IN PARADISE

Words and Music by
PHIL COLLINS

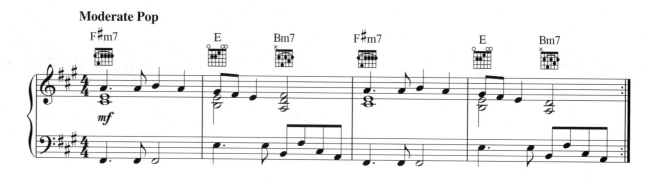

BACK AT ONE

Words and Music by
BRIAN McKNIGHT

BEACH BABY

Words and Music by JOHN CARTER
and GILL SHAKESPEARE

Ah _____

Ah _____   Ah _____   Ah

Do you re-mem-ber back in old L. A. _____ o _____ oh

when ev-'ry-bod-y drove a Chev-ro-let _____ o _____ oh.

64

BEHIND BLUE EYES

Words and Music by
PETE TOWNSHEND

BIG GIRLS DON'T CRY

Words and Music by BOB CREWE
and BOB GAUDIO

BLAZE OF GLORY

Words and Music by
JON BON JOVI

BROWN EYED GIRL

Words and Music by
VAN MORRISON

Additional Lyrics

2. Whatever happened to Tuesday and so slow
Going down the old mine with a transistor radio
Standing in the sunlight laughing
Hiding behind a rainbow's wall
Slipping and a-sliding
All along the water fall
With you, my brown eyed girl
You, my brown eyed girl.
Do you remember when we used to sing:
Chorus

3. So hard to find my way, now that I'm all on my own
I saw you just the other day, my, how you have grown
Cast my memory back there, Lord
Sometime I'm overcome thinking 'bout
Making love in the green grass
Behind the stadium
With you, my brown eyed girl
With you, my brown eyed girl.
Do you remember when we used to sing:
Chorus

BORDERLINE

Words and Music by
REGGIE LUCAS

BRICK

Words and Music by BEN FOLDS
and DARREN JESSEE

94

CALIFORNIA DREAMIN'

Words and Music by JOHN PHILLIPS
and MICHELLE PHILLIPS

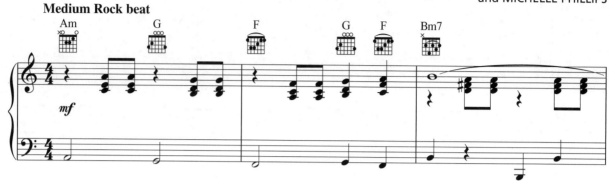

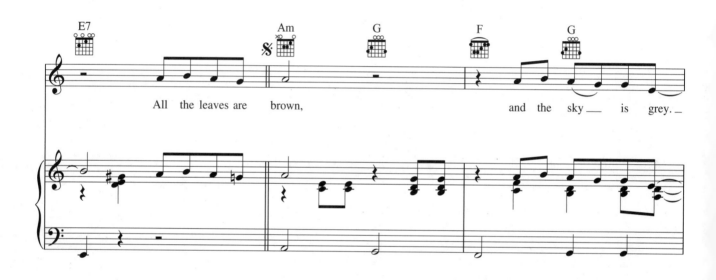

All the leaves are brown, and the sky — is grey. —

I've been — for a walk

98

CAN'T BUY ME LOVE

Words and Music by JOHN LENNON
and PAUL McCARTNEY

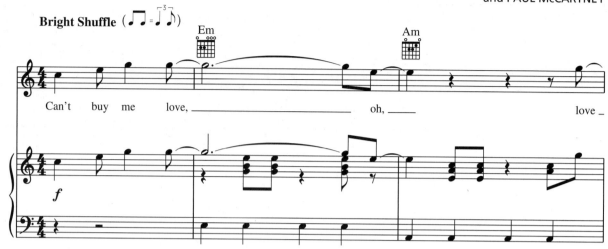

D.S. al Coda

mon - ey can't buy me love. _____ (Scream)

CODA

mon - ey can't buy me love. __ Can't buy me love _____

love _____ can't buy me love. _

CARIBBEAN QUEEN
(No More Love on the Run)

Words and Music by KEITH VINCENT ALEXANDER
and BILLY OCEAN

CHANGES

Words and Music by
DAVID BOWIE

1. I still don't know what I ___ was
2. *(See additional lyrics)*

wait-ing for and my time was run-ning wild. A mil-lion dead - end streets, and

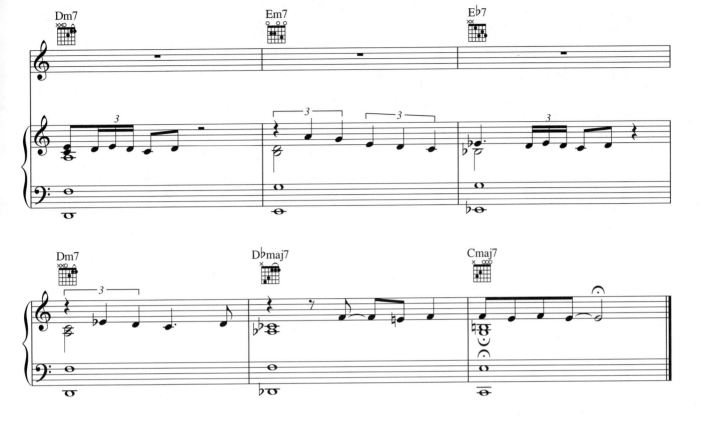

Additional Lyrics

2. I watch the ripples change their size, but never leave the stream
   Of warm impermanence and so the days flowed through my eyes
   But still the days seem the same.
   And these children that you spit on as they try to change their worlds
   Are immune to your consultations, they're quite aware of what they're going through.

   (Ch-ch-ch-ch-Changes) Turn and face the strange.
   (Ch-ch-changes) Don't tell them to grow up and out of it.
   (Ch-ch-ch-ch-Changes) Turn and face the strange.
   (Ch-ch-changes) Where's your shame? You've left us up to our necks in it.
   Time may change me, but you can't trace time.

CLOCKS

Words and Music by GUY BERRYMAN, JON BUCKLAND,
WILL CHAMPION and CHRIS MARTIN

And noth - ing else com - pares. _____

THE CLOSER I GET TO YOU

Words and Music by JAMES MTUME
and REGGIE LUCAS

THE COLOUR OF LOVE

Words and Music by BILLY OCEAN,
JOLYON SKINNER, BARRY EASTMOND
and WAYNE BRATHWAITE

126

128

130

CRAZY IN LOVE

Words and Music by RICH HARRISON,
SHAWN CARTER and BEYONCE KNOWLES

Additional Lyrics

Rap: Young Hov, y'all know when the flow is loco.
Young B and the R-O-C, uh-oh.
Ol' G, big homey, the one and only.
Stick bony, but the pocket is fat like Tony Soprano.
The ROC handle like Van Axel.
I shake phonies, man, you can't get next to the genuine article, I do not sing low.
I sling though, if anything I bling yo'.
A star like Ringo, roar like a gringo.
Bret if you're crazy, bring your whole set.
Jay-Z in the range, crazy and deranged.
They can't figure him out, they like "Hey, is he insane?"
Yes sir, I'm cut from a different cloth.
My texture is the best fur chinchilla.
I been healin' the chain smokers.
How you think I got the name Hova?
I been realer, the game's over.
Fall back young, ever since the label changed over to platinum the game's been a wrap, one.

COME SAIL AWAY

Words and Music by
DENNIS DeYOUNG

COME TO MY WINDOW

Words and Music by
MELISSA ETHERIDGE

Come to my win - dow. Crawl in - side, wait by the light of the moon.

Come to my win - dow. I'll be home soon.

148

COULD IT BE MAGIC

Inspired by "Prelude in C Minor" by F. Chopin

Words and Music by BARRY MANILOW
and ADRIENNE ANDERSON

154

CRYING

Words and Music by ROY ORBISON
and JOE MELSON

DANCING QUEEN

Words and Music by BENNY ANDERSSON,
BJORN ULVAEUS and STIG ANDERSON

160

Watch that ___ scene, ___ dig-gin' the danc - ing ___ queen. ___

Dig - gin' the

danc - ing ___ queen. _____

Repeat and Fade

DANCING WITH MYSELF

Words and Music by BILLY IDOL
and TONY JAMES

B5

elf. If I had ____ the chance, _ I'd ask the

world ____ to dance, _ and if I had ____ the chance, _ I'd ask the

world ____ to dance, _ if I had ____ the chance, _ I'd ask the

world _ to dance. _____ Oh, oh, oh,

DANIEL

Words and Music by ELTON JOHN
and BERNIE TAUPIN

Moderately fast

(1.,4.) Dan - iel is trav -
(2.) They say Spain is pret -
(3.) *Instrumental ad lib.*

- 'ling to - night ___ on a plane. ___
- ty, ___ 'though I've nev - er been. ___

174

DO YOU REALLY WANT TO HURT ME

Words and Music by GEORGE O'DOWD, JON MOSS,
MICHAEL CRAIG and ROY HAY

DON'T DO ME LIKE THAT

Words and Music by
TOM PETTY

(1.) I was talk-in' with a friend of mine,
(2.,D.S.) Lis-ten hon-ey, can you see?

said a wom-an had hurt his pride.
Ba-by, it would bur-y me

DOIN' IT
(All for My Baby)

Words and Music by PHIL CODY
and MIKE DUKE

Ear-ly in the morn-in' ___ I'm still in bed. ___
Lat-er in the eve-nin' it's been a bus-y day.

She comes to me with sweet af-fec - tion. ___
She lays her head up - on my wea-ry shoul - der. ___

189

DON'T SPEAK

Words and Music by ERIC STEFANI
and GWEN STEFANI

194

196

DON'T TALK TO STRANGERS

Words and Music by
RICK SPRINGFIELD

200

DONNA

Words and Music by
RITCHIE VALENS

DREAM WEAVER

Words and Music by
GARY WRIGHT

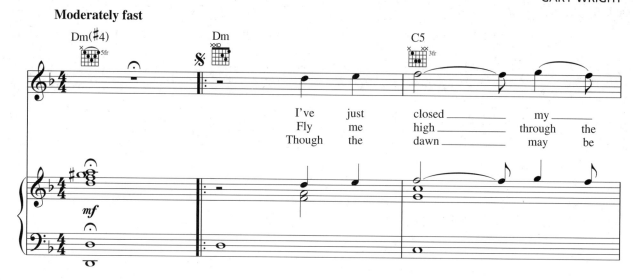

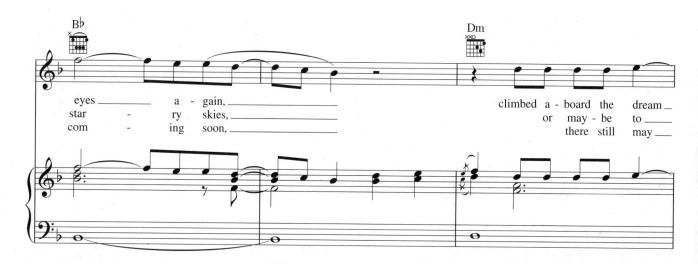

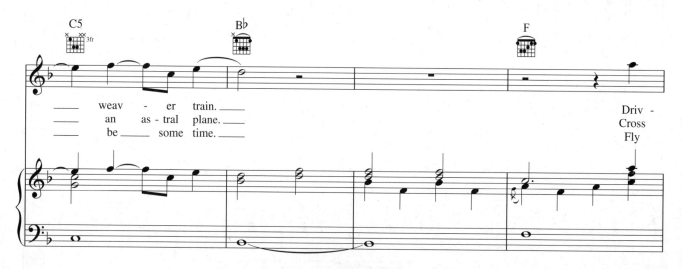

DREAMER

Words and Music by RICK DAVIES
and ROGER HODGSON

Moderately fast

Dream - er, you know you are a dream - er.

Well, can you put your hands in your head, oh no! I said dream - er, you're noth-ing but a

214

you can do some - thing.) If I could do an - y - thing... (But can you do some - thing

out _____ of this world?) _____

Take a dream on a Sun - day.

cresc. little by little

218

Can you put your hands   in your head,   oh   no!   Oh

no!

ELEANOR RIGBY

Words and Music by JOHN LENNON
and PAUL McCARTNEY

Moderately, with a steady beat

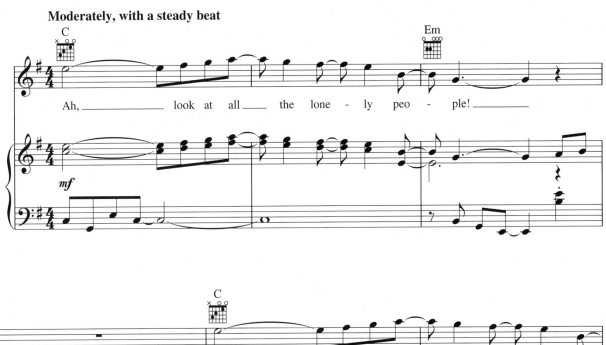

Ah, _____ look at all _____ the lone-ly peo-ple! _____

Ah, _____ look at all _____ the lone-ly peo-

-ple! _____

El - ea - nor Rig - by
Fa - ther Mc - Ken - zie
El - ea - nor Rig - by,

222

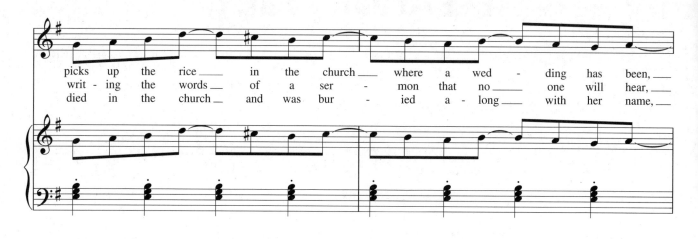

picks up the rice___ in the church___ where a wed - ding has been,___
writ - ing the words___ of a ser - mon that no___ one will hear,___
died in the church___ and was bur - ied a - long___ with her name,___

___ lives in a dream.___ Waits at the win - dow,
___ no one comes near.___ Look at him work - ing,
___ no - bod - y came.___ Fa - ther Mc - Ken - zie,

wear - ing the face___ that she keeps___ in a jar___ by the door,___
darn - ing his socks___ in the night___ when there's no - bod - y there,___
wip - ing the dirt___ from his hands___ as he walks___ from the grave,___

DUST IN THE WIND

Words and Music by
KERRY LIVGREN

ev - 'ry - thing _ is dust in the wind.
wind.)

Repeat and Fade

Optional Ending

poco rit.

EASY

Words and Music by
LIONEL RICHIE

Very slow

Know it sounds fun-ny, but I just can't stand the pain.

Girl, I'm leav - ing you ___ to - mor - row. _____

Seems to me, ___ girl, you know I've done all ___ I can.

231

ENJOY THE SILENCE

Words and Music by
MARTIN GORE

Words_ are ver - y_ un - nec - es - sar - y._ They can on - ly do_

_ harm. _

(percussion)

All I ev - er want - ed,   all I ev - er need - ed __ is here   in   my __

arms.

Words are ver - y___ un - nec - es - sar - y.___

They can on - ly do___ harm.___

Repeat and Fade

Optional Ending

ERES TÚ/TOUCH THE WIND

Words and Music by
JUAN C. CALDERON

242

EVERLASTING LOVE

Words and Music by BUZZ CASON
and MAC GAYDEN

248

EVIL WOMAN

Words and Music by
JEFF LYNNE

EVERY ROSE HAS ITS THORN

Words and Music by BOBBY DALL, BRETT MICHAELS,
BRUCE JOHANNESSON and RIKKI ROCKETT

257

Like the knife that cuts _ you, the wound heals, but the scar, that scar re - mains.

I know I could have saved our love that night _ if I'd

known what to say. _ In - stead of mak - ing love _ we both

made our sepa - rate ways. _ Now I hear you've found some - bod - y new and

EVERYTHING IS BEAUTIFUL

Words and Music by
RAY STEVENS

2. We shouldn't care about the length of his hair or the color of his skin,
   Don't worry about what shows from without but the love that lives within,
   We gonna get it all together now and everything gonna work out fine,
   Just take a little time to look on the good side my friend and straighten it out in your mind.

EXHALE
(Shoop Shoop)
from the Original Soundtrack Album WAITING TO EXHALE

Words and Music by
BABYFACE

(1.) Ev - 'ry - one falls in love some - times. _____ Some - times it's
(2.,3.) laugh, some - times you'll cry. _____ Life nev - er

wrong _____ and some - times it's right. For ev - 'ry
tells __ us _____ the whens or whys. When you've got

win some - one must fail, but there comes a
friends to wish you well, you'll find a

Fallin'

Words and Music by
ALICIA KEYS

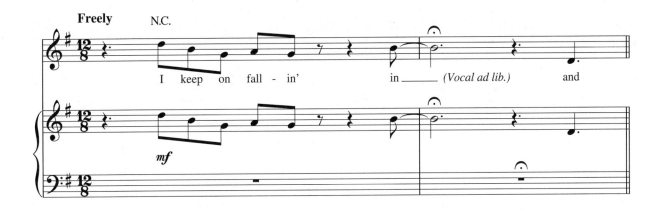

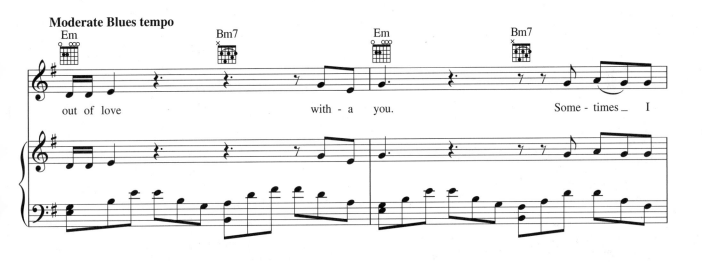

FAST CAR

Words and Music by
TRACY CHAPMAN

Moderately

Play 4 times

You got a fast ___ car. I want a tick-et to an-y-where.
You got a fast ___ car. I got a plan to get us out of here. I've been

May-be we make a deal. ___ May-be to-geth-er we can get some-where. ___
work-ing at the con-ven-ience store. Man-aged to save just a lit-tle bit of mon-ey.

An-y place is bet-ter. ___ Start-ing from ze-ro, got noth-ing to lose.
Won't have to drive too far, just cross the bor-der and in-to the cit-y.

FEELIN' ALRIGHT

Words and Music by
DAVE MASON

FIRE AND ICE

Words and Music by TOM KELLY,
SCOTT SHEETS and PAT BENATAR

by fire and ice.

288

FOOLIN'

Words and Music by JOE ELLIOTT, STEVE CLARK,
PETER WILLIS, RICHARD SAVAGE,
RICHARD ALLEN and ROBERT LANGE

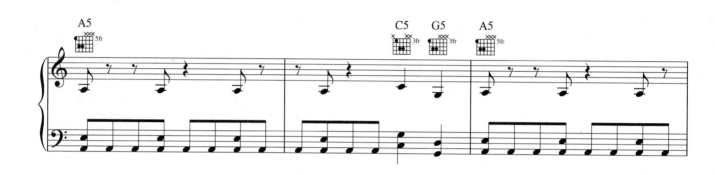

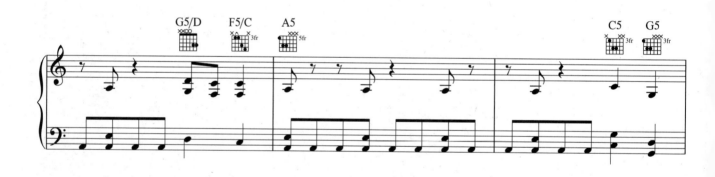

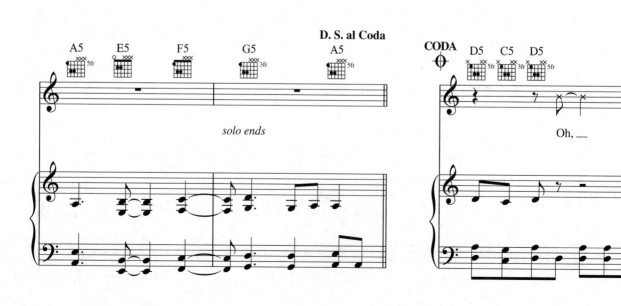

THE FIRST CUT IS THE DEEPEST

Words and Music by
CAT STEVENS

Slowly, with a beat

I would have giv-en you all ___ of my heart, ___ but there's
want ___ you by ___ my side, ___ just to

some-one who's torn it a-part. ___ And {she's}{he's} tak-en just all ___ that I had, ___
help me dry the tears that I've cried. ___ And I'm sure gon-na give you a try, ___

FOOLISH HEART

Words and Music by RANDY GOODRUM
and STEVE PERRY

*Recorded a half step lower.

FOR THE GOOD TIMES

Words and Music by
KRIS KRISTOFFERSON

FREE BIRD

Words and Music by ALLEN COLLINS
and RONNIE VAN ZANT

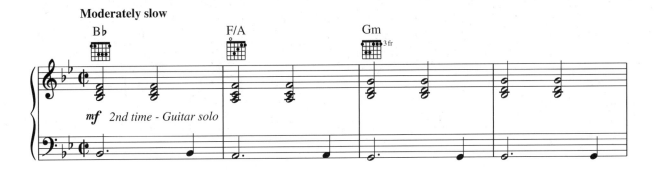

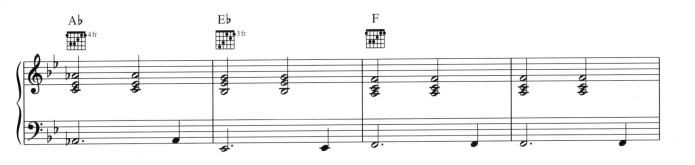

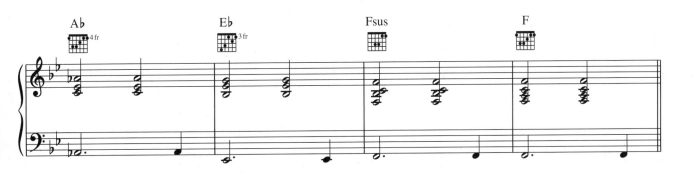

312

GIMME SOME LOVIN'

Words and Music by STEVE WINWOOD,
MUFF WINWOOD and SPENCER DAVIS

Moderately bright

Hey!

Well, my

tem - p'ra - ture's   ris - ing   and my   feet   on   the   floor.
feel   so   good; ___   ev - 'ry - thing   is   sound - ing   hot.
feel   so   good; ___   ev - 'ry - bod - y's   get - tin'   high.

GIVE ME THE NIGHT

Words and Music by
ROD TEMPERTON

Moderately Fast, with funky feeling

mf

1. When-ev-er

Em7 Am7 Bm7 Cmaj7 Em7 Am7 Bm7 Cmaj7

dark is fall - in',
2. *see additional lyrics*
3. *Instrumental*
4. *see additional lyrics*

you know the spir - it of the par - ty starts to come a - live.— Un-til the

Em7 Am7 Bm7 Cmaj7 Em7 Am7 Bm7 Cmaj7

day is dawn - in', you can throw out all the blues— and hit the cit - y— lights,— 'cause there's

320

know we can___ fly?___ So give me the night.   Give me the night.

Give me the night.

___ 4. And if we

Give me the night.

Give me the night.

Give me the night.

Verse 2. You need the evenin' action, a place to dine.
A glass of wine, a little late romance.
It's a chain reaction.
We'll see the people of the world comin' out to dance.
'Cause there's. . . Chorus

Verse 3. (Instrumental)
'Cause there's. . . Chorus

Verse 4. And if we stay together,
We'll feel the rhythm of evening takin' us up high.
Never mind the weather.
We'll be dancin' in the street until the morning light.
'Cause there's. . . Chorus

GOOD VIBRATIONS

Words and Music by BRIAN WILSON
and MIKE LOVE

I _____ Close my eyes, I love the col - or - ful clothes she wears, _____ she's _ some - how clo - ser now. _____

and _ the way the sun - light plays up - on her
Soft - ly smile, I know she must be

hair. _____
kind. _____ Then _____ I _____ hear the sound of a I look

GOOD TIMES

Words and Music by NILE RODGERS
and BERNARD EDWARDS

HALLELUJAH

Words and Music by
LEONARD COHEN

Additional Lyrics

2. Your faith was strong, but you needed proof.
   You saw her bathing on the roof.
   Her beauty and the moonlight overthrew you.
   She tied you to a kitchen chair.
   She broke your throne; she cut your hair.
   And from your lips she drew the Hallelujah. *(To Chorus)*

3. Maybe I have been here before.
   I know this room; I've walked this floor.
   I used to live alone before I knew you.
   I've seen your flag on the marble arch.
   Love is not a victory march.
   It's a cold and it's a broken Hallelujah. *(To Chorus)*

4. There was a time you let me know
   What's real and going on below.
   But now you never show it to me, do you?
   And remember when I moved in you,
   The holy dark was movin' too,
   And every breath we drew was Hallelujah. *(To Chorus)*

5. Maybe there's a God above,
   And all I ever learned from love
   Was how to shoot at someone who outdrew you.
   And it's not a cry you can hear at night.
   It's not somebody who's seen the light.
   It's a cold and it's a broken Hallelujah. *(To Chorus)*

HAPPY TOGETHER

Words and Music by GARRY BONNER
and ALAN GORDON

Imagine me and you, _ I do. I think about you
call you up, _ invest a dime, and you say you be-

day and night. _ It's only right, to think about the girl you love _ and hold her
long to me _ and ease my mind, imagine how the world could be _ so very

tight, so happy together. _ If I should
fine, so happy to-

HAVE I TOLD YOU LATELY

Words and Music by
VAN MORRISON

HAVE YOU EVER SEEN THE RAIN?

Words and Music by
JOHN FOGERTY

Shin-in' down_ like wa-ter._

CHORUS

I want to know,_____ Have you ev-er_ seen the rain?

I want to know,_____ Have you ev-er_ seen the rain

To Coda

com-in' down_ on a sun-ny day?_

HEART OF GLASS

Words and Music by DEBORAH HARRY
and CHRIS STEIN

could've made   it   cruis - ing,   yeah. _____

THE HEAT IS ON
from the Paramount Motion Picture BEVERLY HILLS COP

Words by KEITH FORSEY
Music by HAROLD FALTERMEYER

The heat is on, on _____ the street, _____ in-side your head, on ev - 'ry beat. _____

358

HIGHER LOVE

Words and Music by WILL JENNINGS
and STEVE WINWOOD

366

woah. ___ Bring me a high - er ___ love,

bring me a high - er ___ love. ___

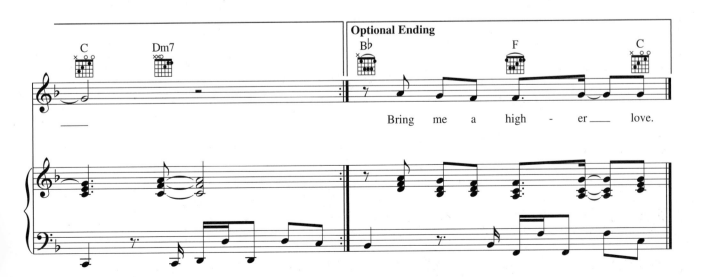

Optional Ending

___ Bring me a high - er ___ love.

HOLD ON LOOSELY

Words and Music by DON BARNES,
JEFF CARLISI and JAMES MICHAEL PETERIK

HOT HOT HOT

Words and Music by
ALPHONSUS CASSELL

Moderate Latin Dance

O - lé, o - lé, o - lé, o - lé. O - lé, o - lé, o -

lé, o - lé.

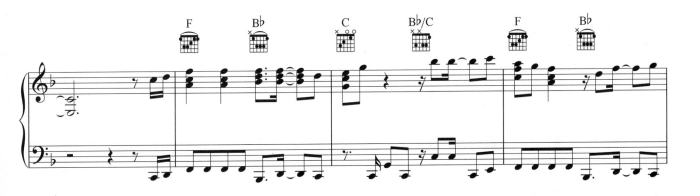

THE HOUSE OF THE RISING SUN

Words and Music by
ALAN PRICE

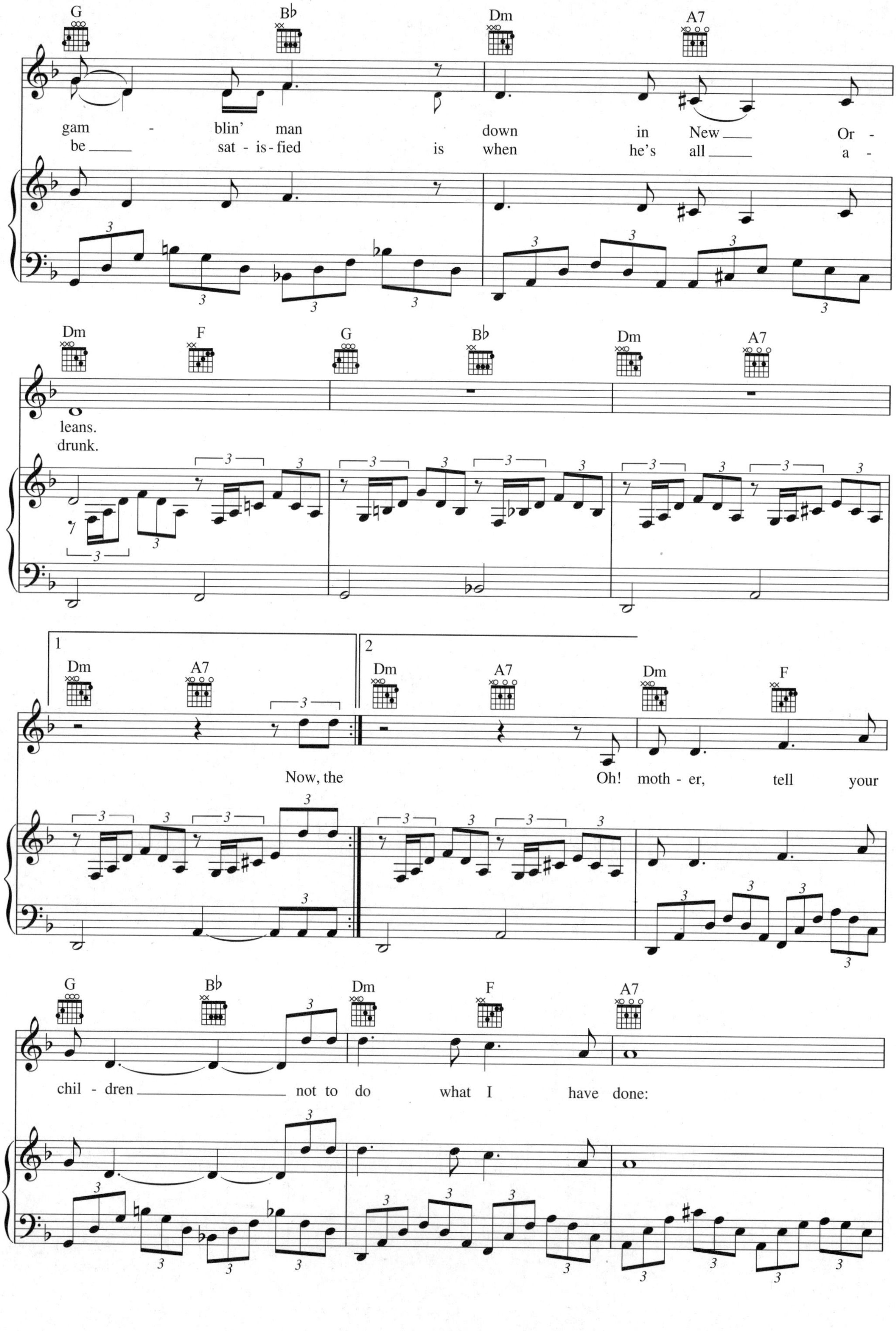

G Bb Dm A7
gam - blin' man down in New Or -
be sat - is - fied is when he's all a -
Dm F G Bb Dm A7
leans.
drunk.
1 2
Dm A7 Dm A7 Dm F
Now, the
Oh! moth - er, tell your
G Bb Dm F A7
chil - dren not to do what I have done:

HOW SWEET IT IS
(To Be Loved by You)

Words and Music by EDWARD HOLLAND,
LAMONT DOZIER and BRIAN HOLLAND

I BELIEVE I CAN FLY

Words and Music by
ROBERT KELLY

I CAN'T GO FOR THAT

Words and Music by DARYL HALL,
JOHN OATES and SARA ALLEN

can't go for that, _ no, _____ no can do. I _____

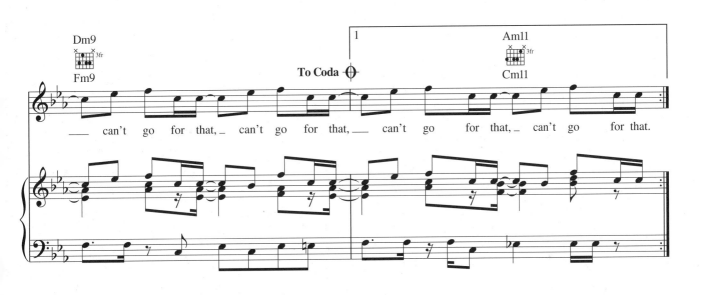

_____ can't go for that, _ can't go for that, _____ can't go for that, _ can't go for that.

_____ can't go for that, _ can't go for that.   can't go for that, _ can't go for that. _

I CAN'T HELP MYSELF

(Sugar Pie, Honey Bunch)

Words and Music by BRIAN HOLLAND,
LAMONT DOZIER and EDWARD HOLLAND

Moderately fast

Su - gar - pie hon - ey bunch, you know that I
Su - gar - pie hon - ey bunch,

love you. __ I can't help my - self,
man should be. I'm weak - er than a
love you. __ I can't help my - self,
man should be.

I DON'T WANT TO WAIT

Words and Music by
PAULA COLE

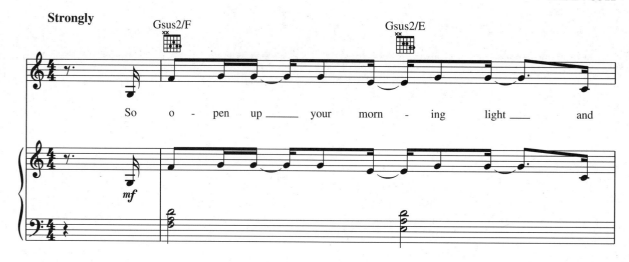

So o- pen up ___ your morn- ing light ___ and

say a lit- tle prayer_ for I. ___ You know that if we are ___ to stay ___ a- live,___ then

see the peace _ in ev- 'ry eye. ___ Du du du ___ du du,

402

403

404

I FINALLY FOUND SOMEONE

Words and Music by BARBRA STREISAND, MARVIN HAMLISCH,
ROBERT LANGE and BRYAN ADAMS

Male: I fi-n'lly found some-one who knocks me off my feet.

I fi-n'lly found the one ___ that makes me feel com-plete.

Female: It start-ed o-ver cof-fee. We start-ed out as friends.

Cm7

Cm7/F

It's fun-ny how from sim-ple things __ the best things be - gin. ____

G

Em7

__ *Male:* This time it's dif - f'rent. It's all be-cause of you. __

Cmaj7

Cm

It's bet - ter than it's ev - er been __ 'cause we can talk it through.

G(add9)

Em7

Female: My fav - 'rite line ____ was, "Can I call you some - time?" __

411

I WANNA GO BACK

Words and Music by MONTY BYROM,
IRA WALKER and DANIEL CHAUNCEY

I re - call __ was list - 'nin' to the ra - di - o. _____
hang - in' out on Fri - day night. _____

I HOPE YOU DANCE

Words and Music by TIA SILLERS
and MARK D. SANDERS

hope you nev - er lose _____ your sense of the won - der.
nev - er fear _____ those _ moun - tains in the dis - tance.

I WANT IT THAT WAY

Words and Music by MARTIN SANDBERG
and ANDREAS CARLSSON

I WILL REMEMBER YOU

Theme from THE BROTHERS McMULLEN

Words and Music by SARAH McLACHLAN,
SEAMUS EGAN and DAVE MERENDA

434

I WILL SURVIVE

Words and Music by DINO FEKARIS
and FREDERICK J. PERREN

I WOULDN'T WANT TO BE LIKE YOU

Words and Music by ALAN PARSONS
and ERIC WOOLFSON

Medium Disco-Rock

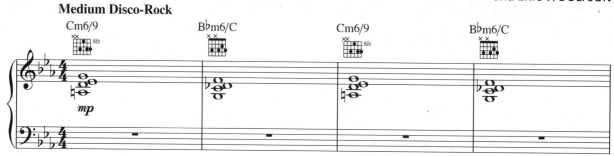

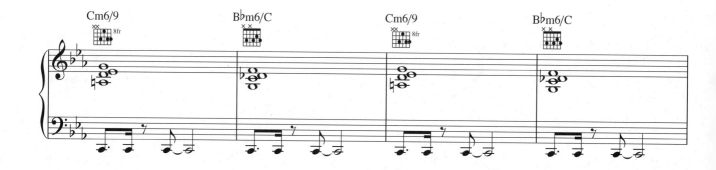

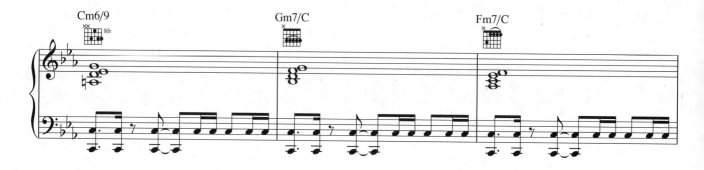

Back on the bot-tom line, _

445

I'D LOVE TO CHANGE THE WORLD

Words and Music by
ALVIN LEE

them and us, ___   stop the war. ___

D.S. al Coda

I'd

CODA

rit.

IF YOU LEAVE ME NOW

Words and Music by
PETER CETERA

IF

Words and Music by
DAVID GATES

IF YOU LOVE SOMEBODY SET THEM FREE

Music and Lyrics by
STING

Free, free, set them free. Free, free, set

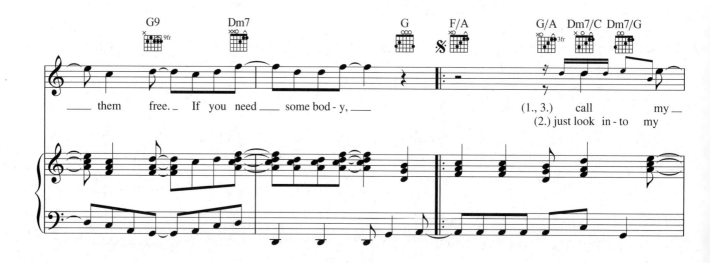

them free. If you need somebody,

(1., 3.) call my
(2.) just look in-to my

name.
eyes,

If you want some-one,
or a whip-ping boy,

INCENSE AND PEPPERMINTS

Words and Music by JOHN CARTER
and TIM GILBERT

IRIS

Words and Music by
JOHN RZEZNIK

IT'S GONNA BE ME

Words and Music by MARTIN SANDBERG,
ANDREAS CARLSSON and RAMI YACOUB

Moderately slow ♩ = 82

(It's gon-na be me.)   Oo, yeah.___

Verse:

1. You might've been hurt, babe, that ain't no lie.___
2. *See additional lyrics*

You've seen them all come and___ go,___ oh.___

482

Verse 2:
You've got no choice, babe,
But to move on, you know
There ain't no time to waste,
'Cause you're just too blind to see.
But in the end you know it's gonna be me.
You can't deny,
So just tell me why...
(To Chorus:)

IT'S MY LIFE

Words and Music by MARK DAVID HOLLIS
and TIM FRESE-GREENE

Moderately fast

It's fun-ny how _ I _____ find _ my-self _ in love _

_ with you. _

If I _____ could buy _ my _____ rea - son-ing, _

* Recorded a half step lower.

IT'S MY TURN

Words by CAROLE BAYER SAGER
Music by MICHAEL MASSER

Slowly, with expression

And if liv-ing for my-self is what I'm guilt-y of, go on and sen-tence me, I'll still be free. It's my turn to see what I can see, I hope you'll un-der-stand,

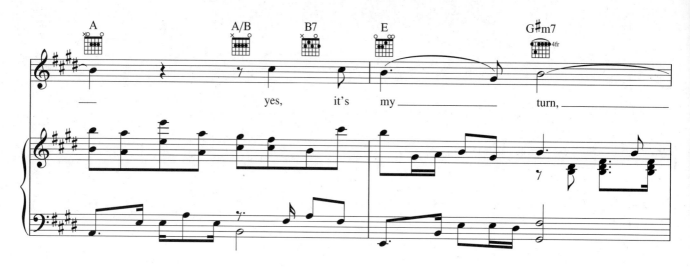

yes, it's my _____ turn, _____

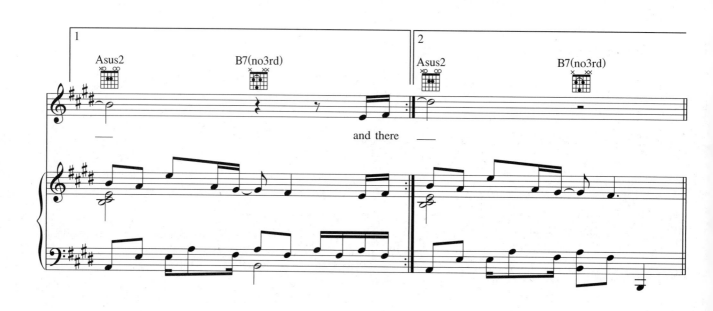

and there ___

(lead vocal ad lib.)
(background vocals) Yes, it's my turn right now!

Repeat ad lib. and Fade

JACK AND DIANE

Words and Music by
JOHN MELLENCAMP

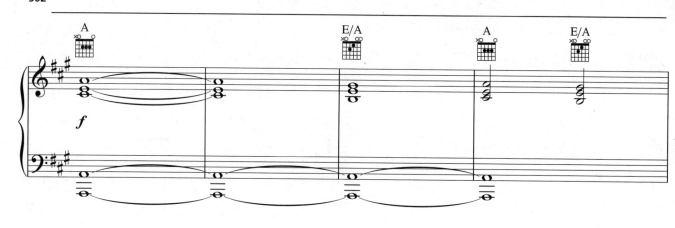

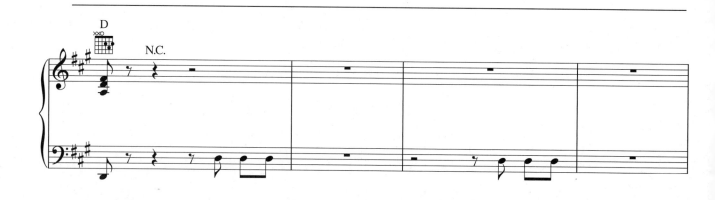

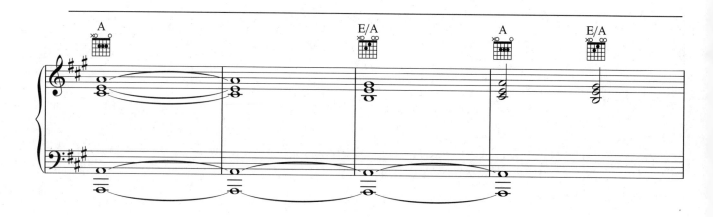

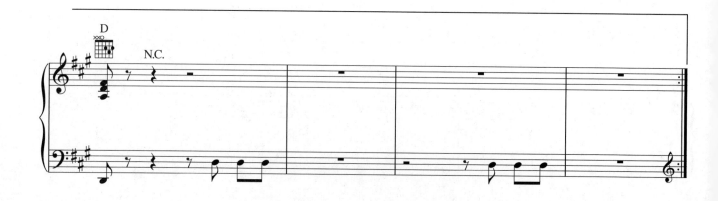

change is com - in' 'round real soon, make us wom - en and men.

C   E/A   D/A   E/A

A   E/A   D/A   A

D.S. al Coda

CODA

A   E

A lit - tle

IT'S TOO LATE

Words and Music by CAROLE KING
and TONI STERN

it, oh, _____ no, ____ no, _____

no, _____ no, ____ no, _____ no.

To Coda

Repeat ad lib.

There'll be good times _ a-gain for me and _ you, _ but we just can't stay to-geth - er; don't you

THE JOKER

Words and Music by STEVE MILLER,
EDDIE CURTIS and AHMET ERTEGUN

Moderately

Some peo-ple call me ___ the Space Cow-boy,   yeah. ___

___ Some call me the Gang-ster of Love. ___

Some peo-ple call me ___ Maur - ice   'cause I

You're the cut - est thing _ that I ev -

- er did see. _____ I real - ly love _ your peach - es, wan - na

LANDSLIDE

Words and Music by
STEVIE NICKS

522

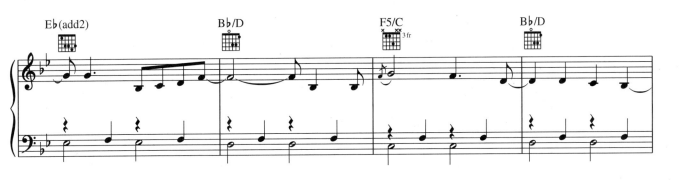

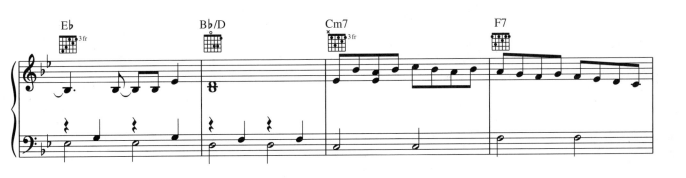

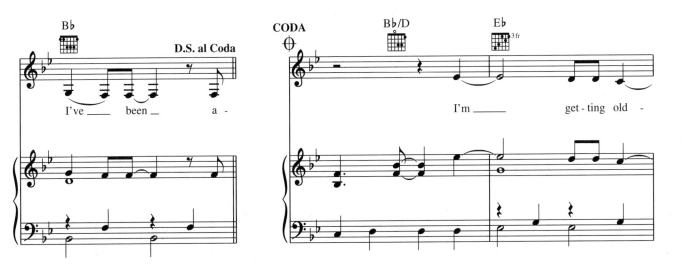

I've __ been __ a-

I'm _____ get-ting old -

JUMP

Words and Music by DAVID LEE ROTH, EDWARD VAN HALEN,
ALEX VAN HALEN and MICHAEL ANTHONY

Bright Rock

530

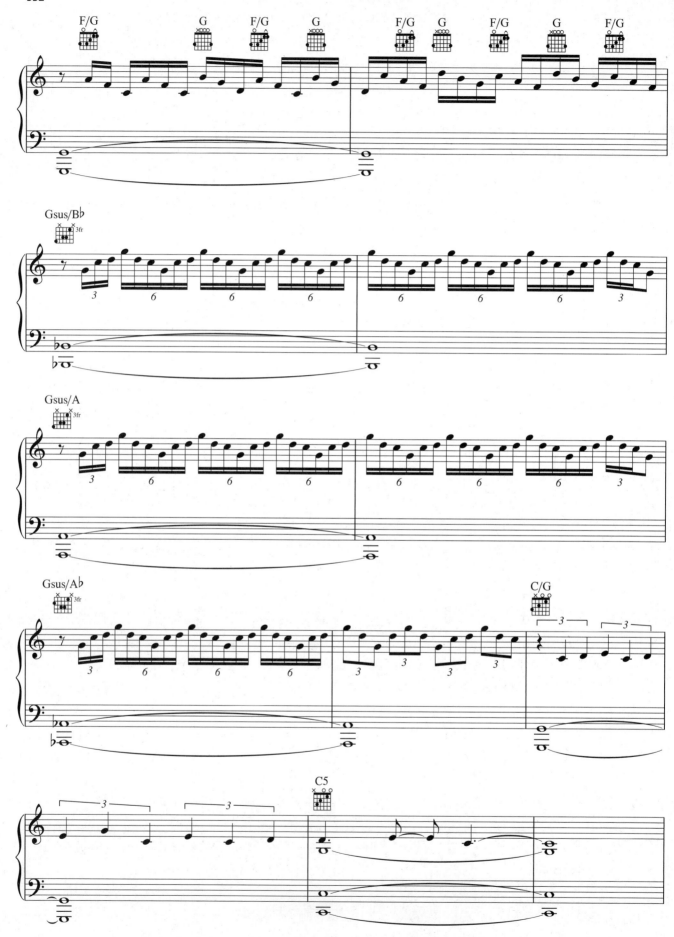

JUST ONE LOOK

Words and Music by DORIS PAYNE
and GREGORY CARROLL

KEEP ON LOVING YOU

Words and Music by
KEVIN CRONIN

LEADER OF THE BAND

Words and Music by
DAN FOGELBERG

An on- ly child a- lone __ and wild, __ a cab- 'net mak- er's son, __
A qui- et man of mu - sic __ de- nied a sim- pler fate, __

543

544

549

LIVIN' LA VIDA LOCA

Words and Music by ROBI ROSA
and DESMOND CHILD

555

THE LOCO-MOTION

Words and Music by GERRY GOFFIN
and CAROLE KING

Moderately fast

Ev-'ry-bod-y's do - ing a brand-new dance ___ now. ___

(Come on, ba-by, do ___ the Lo-co-mo - tion.) I

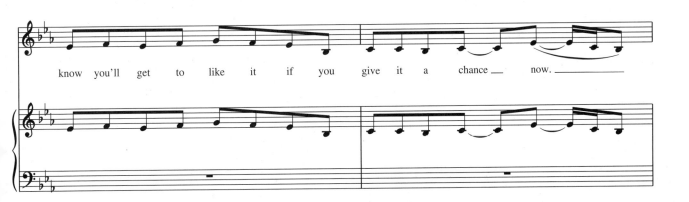

know you'll get to like it if you give it a chance ___ now. ___

LIVIN' ON A PRAYER

Words and Music by JON BON JOVI,
RICHIE SAMBORA and DESMOND CHILD

Moderate Rock

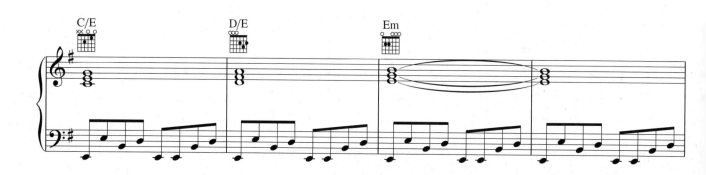

(Spoken:) Once upon a time, not so long ago...

Tom - my used to work on the docks, _____ un - ion's been on strike. He's
Tom - my's got his six-string in hock, _____ now he's hold - ing in what he

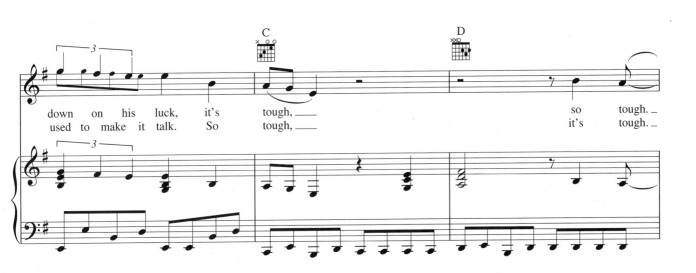

down on his luck, it's tough, _____ so tough. _____
used to make it talk. So tough, _____ it's tough. _____

_____ Gi - na works the di - ner all day _____
_____ Gi - na dreams of run - ning a - way; _____

LOVE THE ONE YOU'RE WITH

Words and Music by
STEPHEN STILLS

Slowly

There's a rose in a fist-ed glove and the

eagle flies with the dove. And

if you can't be with the one you love,

572

LOVE WILL KEEP US TOGETHER

Words and Music by NEIL SEDAKA
and HOWARD GREENFIELD

MINUTE BY MINUTE

Words by MICHAEL McDONALD and LESTER ABRAMS
Music by MICHAEL McDONALD

Hey,__ don't wor - ry. I've been lied __ to.
You __ would stay just to __ watch me, dar - lin',

I've __ been here man - y __ times be - fore.__ Girl, don't you
wilt __ a - way on __ lies from you.__ Can't stop the

LUCY IN THE SKY WITH DIAMONDS

Words and Music by JOHN LENNON
and PAUL McCARTNEY

Moderately

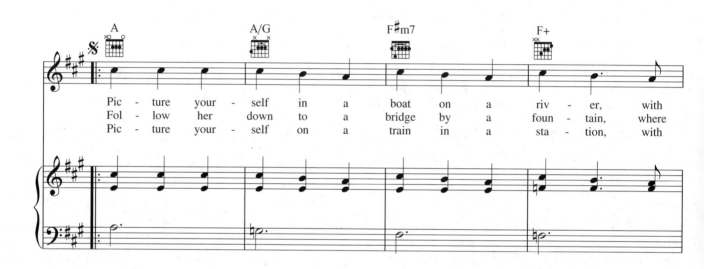

Pic - ture your - self in a boat on a riv - er, with
Fol - low her down to a bridge by a foun - tain, where
Pic - ture your - self on a train in a sta - tion, with

tan - ger - ine trees and mar - ma - lade skies.
rock - ing horse peo - ple eat marsh - mal - low pies.
Plas - ti - cine por - ters with look - ing glass ties.

585

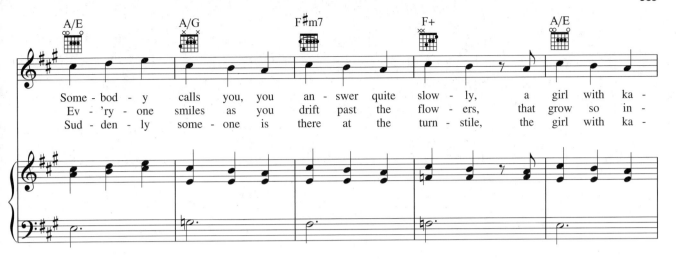

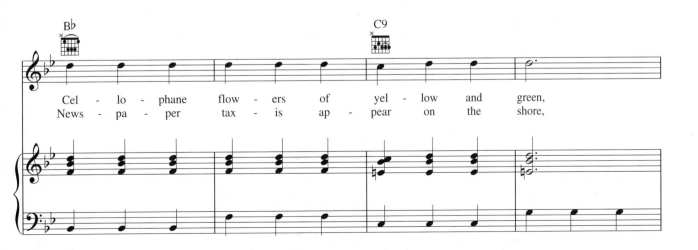

MAN IN THE MIRROR

Words and Music by GLEN BALLARD
and SIEDAH GARRETT

I'm gon-na make a change, _ for once in my _____ life.

It's gon-na feel _ real _ good, _ gon-na make a dif-f'rence, gon-na make it right.

As I turn up the col-lar on __

595

MIDNIGHT BLUE

Words and Music by LOU GRAMM
and BRUCE TURGON

605

MIDNIGHT TRAIN TO GEORGIA

Words and Music by
JIM WEATHERLY

go - in' back   to a sim - pler place and time.

And I'll be with him   on that mid-night train to

Geor - gia.   I'd rath-er live in his world

than live with-out him in mine.

A MOMENT LIKE THIS

Words and Music by JOHN REID
and JORGEN KJELL ELOFSSON

Original key: C# minor. This edition has been transposed up one half-step to be more playable.

Some peo-ple search_ for- ev - er for that one spe - cial kiss._

Oh, I can't be - lieve_ it's hap - pen-ing_ to me._____ Some

peo - ple wait_ a life - time for a mo - ment_ like this. _

Choir: (Mo-ment like this.) _

Lead vocal ad lib.

MY CHERIE AMOUR

Words and Music by STEVIE WONDER,
SYLVIA MOY and HENRY COSBY

621

622

MY LOVE

Words and Music by
PAUL and LINDA McCARTNEY

NEW KID IN TOWN

Words and Music by JOHN DAVID SOUTHER,
DON HENLEY and GLENN FREY

There's talk on the street;__ it sounds so fa-mil - iar.
You look in her eyes;__ the mu - sic be-gins to play.

627

John-ny-come-late - ly, the new kid in town.
John-ny-come-late - ly, the new kid in town.

Ev-'ry-bod-y loves _ you, so don't _ let them down. _
Will she still love _ you

when you're not a - round? _____

There's so man-y things you should have told _ her,

hind ___ you. They will nev - er for - get you till

some-bod - y new comes a - long. ___

Where you been late - ly? There's a new kid in town.

Ev - 'ry-bod - y loves ___ him, don't ___ they? ___ Now he's hold - ing

631

632

NIGHT MOVES

Words and Music by
BOB SEGER

636

Freely

I a-woke last night to the sound of thun-der. How far off, I

sat and won-dered. Start ed hum-ming a song _ from nine-teen six -ty - two. _

Ain't it fun-ny how the night moves? _ When you just don't seem to have as much to lose. _

NOTHING'S GONNA STOP US NOW

Words and Music by DIANE WARREN
and ALBERT HAMMOND

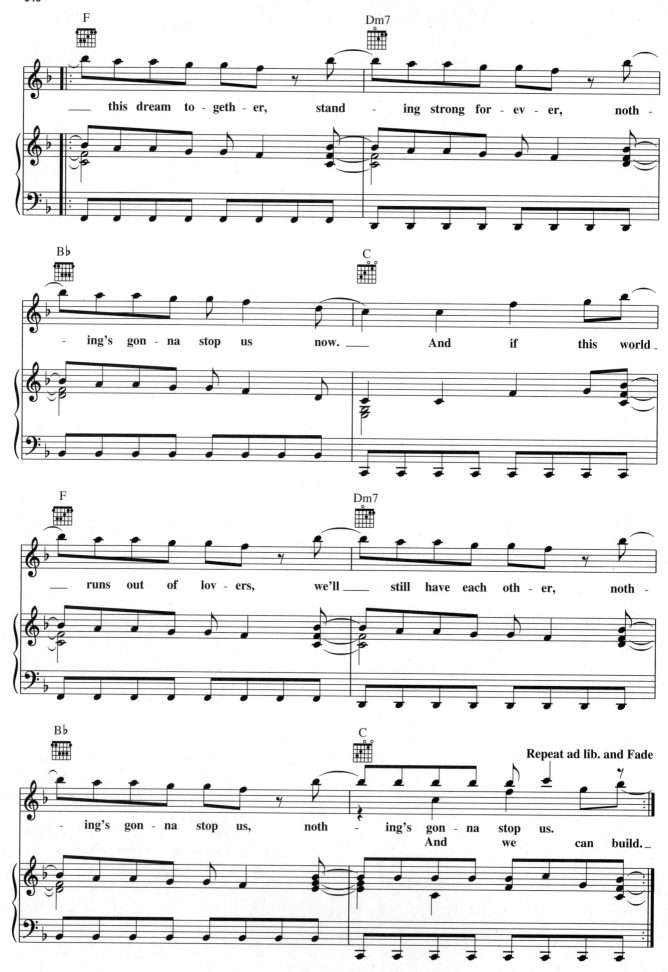

ONE MORE NIGHT

Words and Music by
PHIL COLLINS

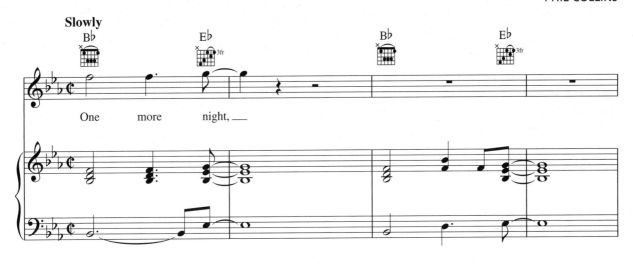

One more night, ___

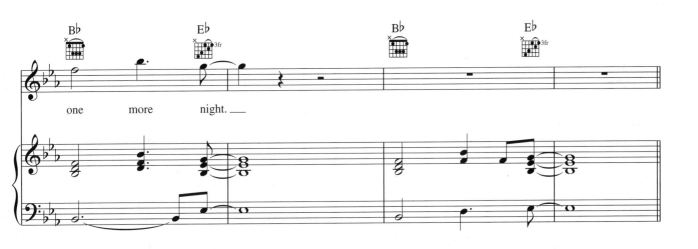

one more night. ___

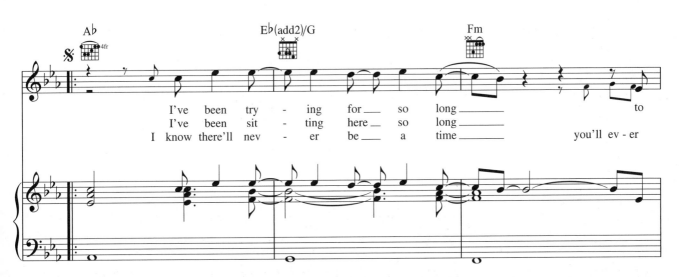

I've been try - ing for ___ so long ___ to

I've been sit - ting here ___ so long ___

I know there'll nev - er be ___ a time ___ you'll ev - er

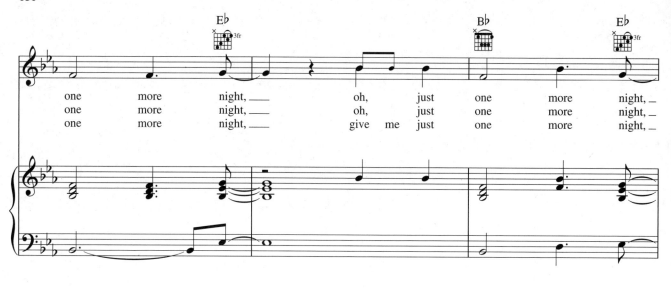

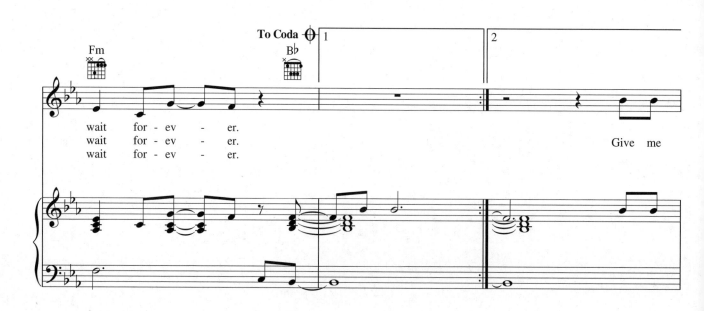

OH SHERRIE

Words and Music by STEVE PERRY, RANDY GOODRUM,
BILL CUOMO and CRAIG KRAMPF

658

ON BROADWAY

Words and Music by BARRY MANN, CYNTHIA WEIL,
MIKE STOLLER and JERRY LEIBER

Moderately, with a beat

Lyrics (verse 1):
They say the ne - on lights are bright __ on Broad - way. __ They say there's al - ways mag - ic in __ the air. __

Lyrics (verse 2):
They say the girls are some - thin' else __ on Broad - way. __ but look - in' at them just gives me __ the blues, __

Lyrics (verse 3):
They say that I won't last too long __ on Broad - way. __ I'll catch a Grey - hound bus for home, __ they say.

ONLY WANNA BE WITH YOU

Words and Music by DARIUS CARLOS RUCKER,
EVERETT DEAN FELBER, MARK WILLIAM BRYAN
and JAMES GEORGE SONEFELD

668

OOO BABY BABY

Words and Music by WILLIAM "SMOKEY" ROBINSON
and WARREN MOORE

OOPS!...I DID IT AGAIN

Words and Music by MARTIN SANDBERG
and RAMI YACOUB

got lost in the game.___ Oh, ba - by, ba - by.

Oops!... You think I'm in love,___ that I'm sent from a - bove.___

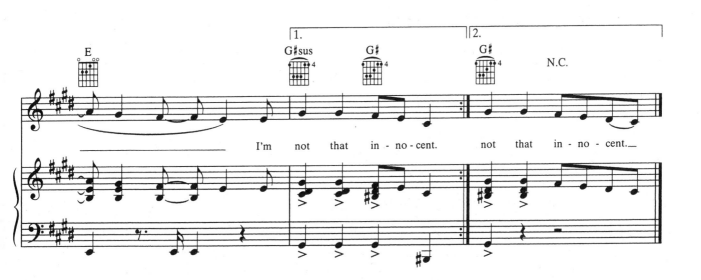

_____ I'm not that in - no - cent. not that in - no - cent.___

OPERATOR
(That's Not the Way It Feels)

Words and Music by
JIM CROCE

REAL LOVE

Words and Music by MARK C. ROONEY,
MARK MORALES and KIRK ROBINSON

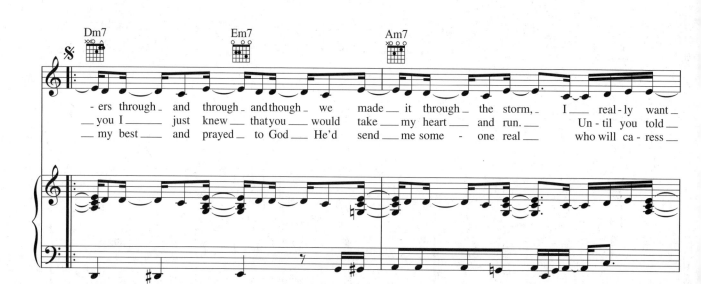

SAILING

Words and Music by
CHRISTOPHER CROSS

694

RIKKI DON'T LOSE THAT NUMBER

Words and Music by WALTER BECKER
and DONALD FAGEN

Moderately

We hear you're leav-ing, that's O.
I have a friend in town, he's heard your

K.
name.

I thought our lit-tle
We can go out

wild time had just be-gun.
driv-ing on _____ Slow Hand Row.

let - ter   to your -   self.

Rik - ki, don't lose that num - ber;   it's the   on - ly   one you   own. ___

___ You might   use it if   you   feel   bet - ter

when you   get _____   home.

ROLL WITH IT

Words and Music by WILL JENNINGS,
STEVE WINWOOD, EDDIE HOLLAND,
LAMONT DOZIER and BRIAN HOLLAND

Medium Funk

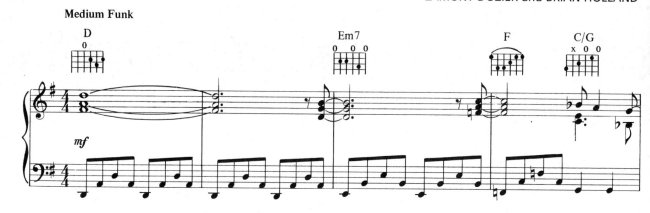

When life____

____ is too much,____ roll with it, ba - by.
way that you love____ is good as mon - ey.
-'ll be a day, you'll get there, ba - by.

Don't
I
You'll

Now there___

Repeat and fade (ad-lib vocal)

SECRET AGENT MAN

from the Television Series

Words and Music by P.F. SLOAN
and STEVE BARRI

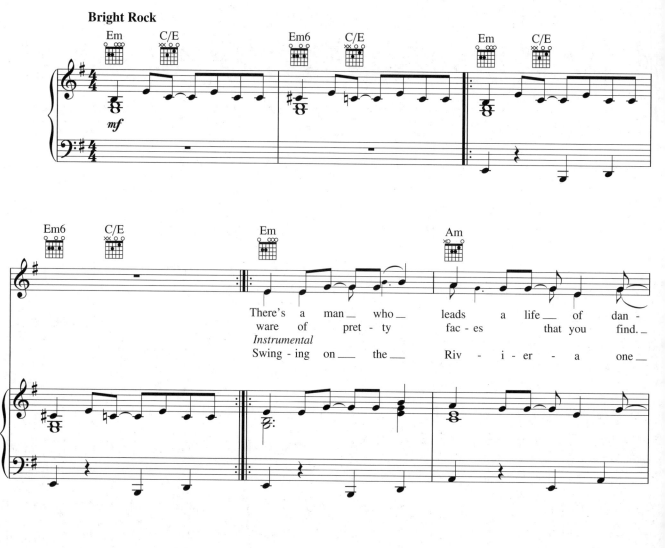

SEXUAL HEALING

Words and Music by MARVIN GAYE,
ODELL BROWN and DAVID RITZ

Let's make love to-night! __ Wake up, wake up,

wake up, wake up, 'cause you do it right! __

Repeat and Fade

SEVEN BRIDGES ROAD

Words and Music by
STEPHEN T. YOUNG

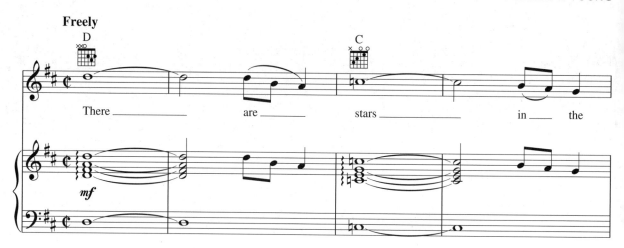

There _____ are _____ stars _____ in _____ the

South - ern sky. _____ And if

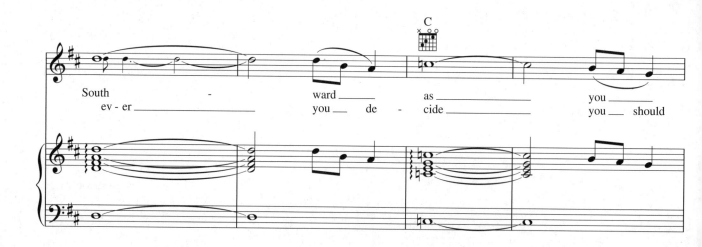

South - ward _____ as _____ you
ev - er _____ you _____ de - cide _____ you _____ should

722

Bright Country

725

SHE WORKS HARD FOR THE MONEY

Words and Music by DONNA SUMMER
and MICHAEL OMARTIAN

She al - read - y knows ____ these are the good times.

She'll nev - er sell out. ____ She nev - er will, ____

not for a dol - lar bill. She works hard ____

D.S. and Fade

SHE'S A BEAUTY

Words and Music by STEVEN LUKATHER, DAVID FOSTER,
JOHN WAYBILL and BILL SPOONER

737

SHE'S LIKE THE WIND

Music and Lyrics by PATRICK SWAYZE
and STACY WIDELITZ

Slowly

She's like the wind___ through my tree.

She rides the night___ next to me. She

leads me through moon - light on - ly to burn___ me with the sun. She's

SHOULD'VE NEVER LET YOU GO

Words and Music by NEIL SEDAKA
and PHIL CODY

1. When you walk in-to a room,
2. stakes
3. room,

your beau-ty steals my breath a-way. ____
and we both have made our share. ____
You know I stand on shak-y ground. ____

When you look in-to my eyes, ____ I find it
but a life with-out your love ____ is a
I've built so man-y walls a-round ____ me, now the

SMOOTH

Words by ROB THOMAS
Music by ROB THOMAS and ITAAL SHUR

SMOOTH OPERATOR

Words and Music by HELEN ADU
and RAY ST. JOHN

SOMEWHERE OUT THERE
from AN AMERICAN TAIL

Words and Music by JAMES HORNER,
BARRY MANN and CYNTHIA WEIL

764

STAGES

Words and Music by BILLY F GIBBONS,
DUSTY HILL and FRANK BEARD

768

SON-OF-A-PREACHER MAN

Words and Music by JOHN HURLEY
and RONNIE WILKINS

THE SPACE BETWEEN

Words and Music by DAVID J. MATTHEWS
and GLEN BALLARD

Additional Lyrics

2. The rain that falls splashed in your heart,
   Ran like sadness down the window into your room.

3. The space between our wicked lies is where
   We hope to keep safe from pain.

4. Take my hand 'cause
   We're walking out of here.

5. Oh, right out of here.
   Love is all we need, dear.

SPINNING WHEEL

Words and Music by
DAVID CLAYTON THOMAS

START ME UP

Words and Music by MICK JAGGER
and KEITH RICHARDS

788

(Just Like)
STARTING OVER

Words and Music by
JOHN LENNON

Our life to-geth-er is so pre-cious to-

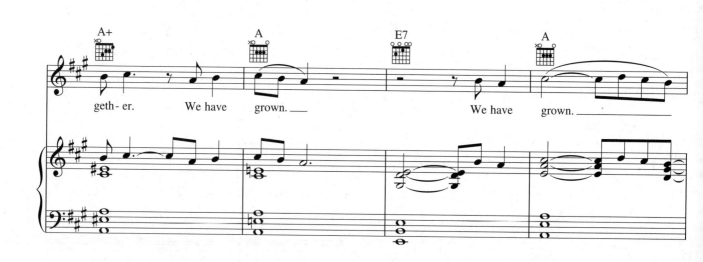

geth-er. We have grown. We have grown.

Al-though our love is still spe-cial,

STUCK IN THE MIDDLE WITH YOU

Words and Music by GERRY RAFFERTY
and JOE EGAN

(1.) Well, I don't

know why I came here to - night. ___ I got the

stuck in the mid - dle with you ___ and I'm won -

Tryin' to make some sense of it all ___ but I can see ___

Instrumental

798

CODA

Lyrics:
And I don't __ know why I came here to - night. __
I got the feel - in' that some - thing ain't right. __ I'm so scared __
in case I fall off my chair __ and I'm won - d'ring how I'll get down the stairs. __

STAY

Words and Music by
LISA LOEB

STEPPIN' OUT

Words and Music by
JOE JACKSON

Recorded a half step higher.

812

STRAIGHT UP

Words and Music by
ELLIOT WOLFF

STRONG ENOUGH

Words and Music by KEVIN GILBERT,
DAVID BAERWALD, SHERYL CROW,
BRIAN McLEOD, BILL BOTTRELL
and DAVID RICKETTS

1. God I feel like___ hell to-
2. Noth-ing's true and___ noth-ing's
3. I have a face I___ can-not
4. When I've shown you that I___ just don't

night, the tears of rage I___ can-not fight.
right, so let me be a-lone to-night.
show, I make the rules up___ as I go.
care. When I'm throw-ing punch-es___ in the air.

823

but   please,_____   don't   leave._____

leave._____

SUPERMAN
(It's Not Easy)

Words and Music by
JOHN ONDRASIK

ooh,   ooh, ____   ooh. _____   It's   not   eas -

- y _____   to   be ____   me.

SURRENDER

Words and Music by
RICK NIELSEN

SWEET DREAMS ARE MADE OF THIS

Words and Music by DAVID A. STEWART
and ANNIE LENNOX

Moderately steady beat

Sweet dreams are made __
Instrumental

__ of this. __ Who am __ I __ to dis - a - gree? __ I

trav - el the world __ and the sev - en seas, __ Ev - 'ry - bod - y's

Hold your head up, mov-in' on. ___ Keep your head up, mov-in' on. ___

Hold your head up, mov-in' on. ___ Keep your head up, mov-in' on. ___

D.S. al Coda

Hold your head up, mov-in' on. ___ Keep your head up.

CODA

SWEET EMOTION

Words and Music by STEVEN TYLER
and TOM HAMILTON

You're call - in' my name but I
Well, I got good news, she's a
You're tell - in' her things but your
I'm talk - in' 'bout some-thin' you can

got - ta make clear. _____ I
real good li - ar, 'cause my
girl - friend lied; _____ you
sure un - der - stand, _____ 'cause a

can't say, ba - by, where I'll be in a year. _____
back - stage boo - gie set your pants on fire. _____
can't catch me 'cause the rab - bit done died. _____
month on the road and I'll be eat - in' from your hand. _____

TAKE ME TO THE RIVER

Words and Music by AL GREEN
and MABON HODGES

851

TAKE MY BREATH AWAY
(Love Theme)
from the Paramount Picture TOP GUN

Words and Music by GIORGIO MORODER
and TOM WHITLOCK

856

TALKING IN YOUR SLEEP

Words and Music by JIMMY MARINOS,
WALLY PALMAR, MIKE SKILL,
COZ CANLER and PETER SOLLEY

1st time only

1
2

When you

close your eyes __ and you go to sleep
hold you in __ my arms at night

TEACH YOUR CHILDREN

Words and Music by
GRAHAM NASH

TEARS IN HEAVEN

Words and Music by ERIC CLAPTON
and WILL JENNINGS

Would you know   my   name _____
Would you hold   my   hand _____
Would you know   my   name _____

if I   saw   you   in   heav - en?
if I   saw   you   in   heav - en?
if I   saw   you   in   heav - en?

Would   it   be   the   same _____
Would   you   help   me   stand _____
Would   you   be   the   same _____

TELL IT LIKE IT IS

Words and Music by GEORGE DAVIS
and LEE DIAMOND

Moderately slow

If ___ you ___ want ___ some-thing to

play ___ with ___ go and find ___ your-self a toy. ___

Ba - by, my time ___ is too ex -

pen - sive,

and I'm not ___ a lit-tle boy. ___

THESE BOOTS ARE MADE FOR WALKIN'

Words and Music by
LEE HAZLEWOOD

Brightly

You keep say - in' ____ you got some - thin'
You keep ly - in' ____ when you ought - a be
You keep play - in' ____ where you should - n't be

for me, some - thin' you call
"truth - in'," you keep los - in'
play - in', you keep think - in'

love but ____ con - fess.
when you ought - a not bet.
that you'll nev - er get burned.

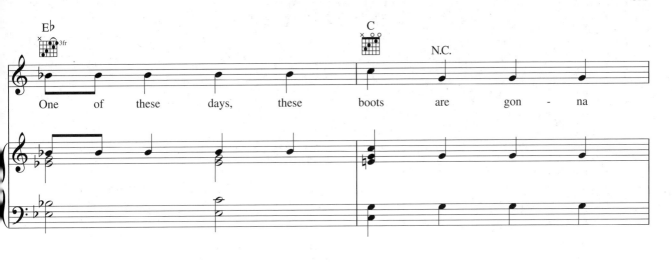

One of these days, these boots are gon - na

walk all____ o - ver you.____

TEMPTED

Words and Music by CHRISTOPHER DIFFORD
and GLENN TILBROOK

Recorded a half step lower.

THAT DON'T IMPRESS ME MUCH

Words and Music by SHANIA TWAIN
and R.J. LANGE

887

THESE DREAMS

Words and Music by MARTIN GEORGE PAGE
and BERNIE TAUPIN

Spare a lit - tle can - dle, save some light for me;
Is it cloak and dag - ger? Could it be spring or fall?
The sweet - est song is si - lence that I've ev - er heard.

fig - ures up a - head mov - ing in the trees. White
I walk with - out a cut through a stained - glass wall,
Fun - ny how your feet in dreams nev - er touch the earth. In a

THIS IS THE NIGHT

Words and Music by GARY BURR,
ALDO NOVA and CHRISTOPHER BRAIDE

When the world was-n't up-side down, ___ I could take all the time ___ I had. ___ But I'm not gon-na wait ___ when a mo-ment can van-ish so fast. ___ 'Cause

E/G#   Asus2   D   Bsus   B

____ of the earth, _ and we'll fly. _____ I've been

C#m7   E/B   A   A/B   E

wait - ing for - ev - er for this, _____ this is the night.

C#m   A   E

This is the night _ where we cap - ture for - ev - er and all ___ our to - mor - rows be - gin. _

Bsus   B   C#m   A

___ Af - ter to - night _ we will nev - er be lone - ly a - gain. _

TIL I HEAR IT FROM YOU

Words and Music by JESSE VALENZUELA,
ROBIN WILSON and MARSHALL CRENSHAW

A THOUSAND MILES

Words and Music by
VANESSA CARLTON

Mak-ing my way down-town, walk-ing fast. Fac-es pass and I'm home-bound.

* Recorded a half step higher.

TIGHTER, TIGHTER

Words and Music by TOMMY JAMES
and ROBERT KING

Tight - er, do do do do, tight - er. Tight - er, do do do do,

tight - er.

You know I got to show you no - bod - y else be - fore you

Just a lit-tle, just a lit-tle, just a lit-tle bit tight - er, now, ba - by.

Just a lit-tle, just a lit-tle, just a lit-tle bit tight - er, now _ babe.

Just a lit-tle, just a lit-tle, just a lit-tle bit tight - er, now, ba - by.

hold on _ a lit-tle bit tight - er, babe. _

TIME AFTER TIME

Words and Music by CYNDI LAUPER
and ROB HYMAN

TO LOVE SOMEBODY

Words and Music by ROBIN GIBB
and BARRY GIBB

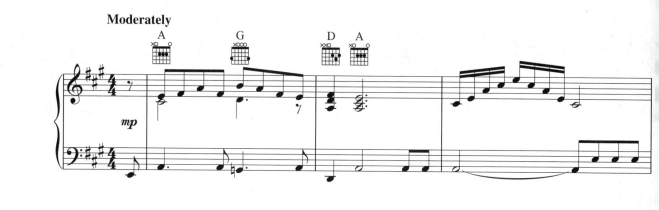

There's a light,   a cer-tain kind of light
brain   I see your face a - gain;

that nev - er shone on me.   I want my life to
I know my frame of mind.   You ain't got to be so

TO LOVE YOU MORE

Words and Music by DAVID FOSTER
and JUNIOR MILES

Slowly, half-time feel

Take me back in-to the arms I love. _____ Need me like you did be - fore. _

TRAIN IN VAIN

Words and Music by MICK JONES
and JOE STRUMMER

TRUE COMPANION

Words and Music by
MARC COHN

D.S. al Coda

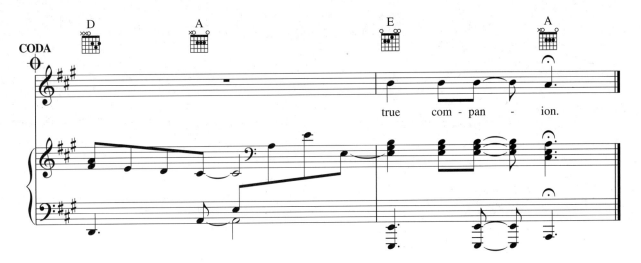

CODA

true com - pan - ion.

2. So don't you dare and try to walk away;
   I've got my heart set on our wedding day.
   I've got this vision of a girl in white,
   Made my decision that it's you all right.
   And when I take your hand,
   I'll watch my heart set sail.
   I'll take my trembling fingers
   And I'll lift up your veil.
   Then I'll take you home,
   And with wild abandon
   Make love to you just like a true companion.
   You are my true companion.
   I got a true companion,
   Woah, a true companion.

3. When the years have done irreparable harm,
   I can see us walking slowly arm in arm,
   Just like that couple on the corner do,
   'Cause girl I will always be in love with you.
   And when I look in your eyes,
   I'll still see that spark,
   Until the shadows fall,
   Until the room grows dark.
   Then when I leave this earth,
   I'll be with the angels standin';
   I'll be out there waiting for my true companion,
   Just for my true companion.
   True companion,
   True companion.

TULSA TIME

Words and Music by
DANNY FLOWERS

WALK AWAY

Words and Music by
JOE WALSH

TURN THE PAGE

Words and Music by
BOB SEGER

fore. _____

But your thoughts will soon be wan-der-in' _____ the

way they al - ways do _____ when you're rid - in' six - teen hours _____ and there's

noth - in' much _____ to do _____ and you don't feel much like rid - in', you just

wish the trip _____ was through. _____

Chorus

Say, here I

2. Well, you ___ Here I

D.S. al Coda

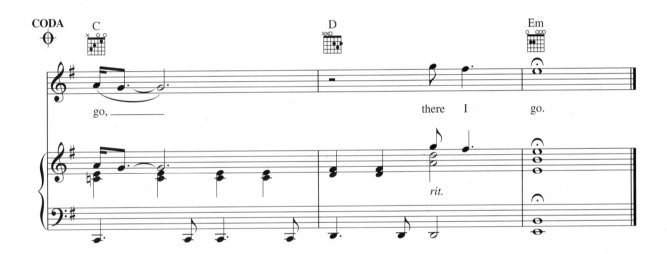

CODA

go, ___ there I go.

rit.

Additional Lyrics

2. Well, you walk into a restaurant strung out from the road
And you feel the eyes upon you as you're shakin' off the cold;
You pretend it doesn't bother you but you just want to explode.
Most times you can't hear 'em talk, other times you can,
All the same old cliches, "Is that a woman or a man?"
And you always seem out numbered, you don't dare make a stand.
Chorus

3. Out there in the spotlight you're a million miles away.
Every ounce of energy you try to give away
As the sweat pours out your body like the music that you play.
Later in the evening as you lie awake in bed
With the echoes from the amplifiers ringing in your head,
You smoke the day's last cigarette remembering what she said.
Chorus

WALK AWAY RENEE

Words and Music by MIKE BROWN,
TONY SANSONE and BOB CALILLI

And when I see ___ the sign ___ that points one way, ___
From deep in - side ___ the tears ___ that I forced to cry, ___

___ the lot we used ___ to pass ___ by ev - 'ry day ___
___ from deep in - side ___ the pain ___ that I chose to hide. ___

___ just walk a - way, ___ Re - nee, ___ you won't see me fol - low you ___
___ Just walk a - way, ___ Re - nee, ___ you won't see me fol - low you ___

WALKING ON SUNSHINE

Words and Music by
KIMBERLEY REW

WALK ON BY

Lyric by HAL DAVID
Music by BURT BACHARACH

pri - vate 'cause each time   I   see you,   I break down and   cry.
tears and   the sad - ness   you   gave me   when you   said good - bye.

Walk on   by. ____   Don't   stop!   Walk on   by. ____

____   Don't   stop!   Walk on   by. ____

WALKING IN MEMPHIS

Words and Music by
MARC COHN

982

mid-dle of the pour - ing rain. _____ Touched down _____ in the land of the

Del - ta Blues in the mid-dle of the pour - ing rain.

rit.

a tempo

THE WARRIOR

Words and Music by NICK GILDER
and HOLLY KNIGHT

1. You run, run, run a - way; ___

2. *(See additional lyrics)*

it's your heart that you be - tray.

Feed-ing on your hun-gry eyes,

I bet you're not so civ-i-lized.

Chorus

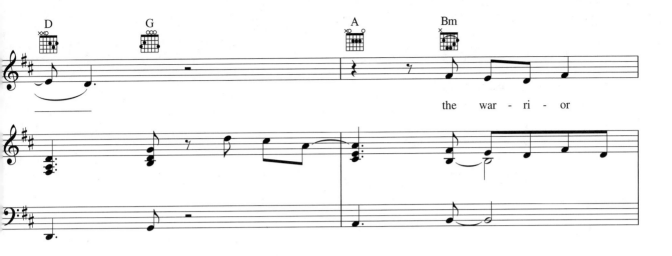

the war – ri – or

the war – ri – or.

D.S. and Fade

Additional Lyrics

2. You talk, talk, you talk to me,
   Your eyes touch me physically.
   Stay with me, we'll take the night
   As passion takes another bite.
   Who's the hunter, who's the game?
   I feel the beat, call your name.
   I hold you close in victory.
   I don't wanna tame your animal style;
   You won't be caged in the call of the wild.
   Chorus

WATERFALLS

Words and Music by MARQUEZE ETHERIDGE,
LISA NICOLE LOPES, RICO R. WADE,
PAT BROWN and RAMON MURRAY

A lone - ly moth - er gaz - ing out of her win - dow star - ing
Lit - tle pre - cious has a nat - 'ral ob - ses - sion for temp -

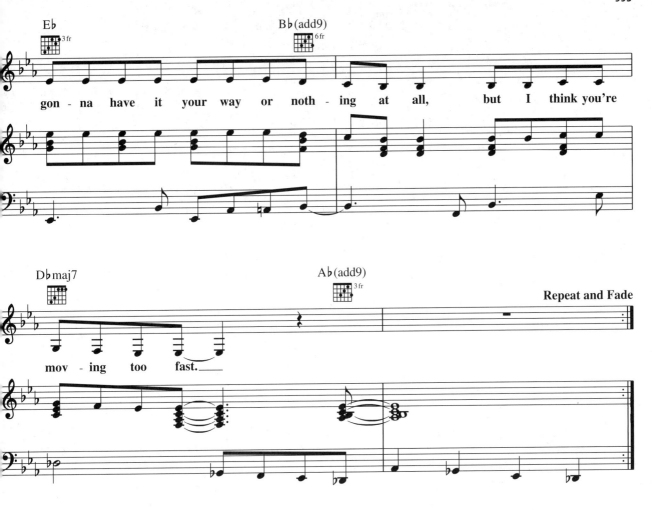

gon - na have it your way or noth - ing at all, but I think you're

mov - ing too fast.

Repeat and Fade

Additional Lyrics

Rap: I seen a rainbow yesterday
But too many storms have come and gone
Leavin' a trace of not one God-given ray
Is it because my life is ten shades of gray
I pray all ten fade away
Seldom praise Him for the sunny days
And like His promise is true
Only my faith can undo
The many chances I blew
To bring my life to anew
Clear blue and unconditional skies
Have dried the tears from my eyes
No more lonely cries
My only bleedin' hope
Is for the folk who can't cope
Wit such an endurin' pain
That it keeps 'em in the pourin' rain
Who's to blame
For tootin' caine in your own vein
What a shame
You shoot and aim for someone else's brain
You claim the insane
And name this day in time
For fallin' prey to crime
I say the system got you victim to your own mind
Dreams are hopeless aspirations
In hopes of comin' true
Believe in yourself
The rest is up to me and you

THE WAY YOU MOVE

Words and Music by ANTWAN PATTON,
PATRICK BROWN and CARLTON MAHONE

Moderate groove

(Rap continues)

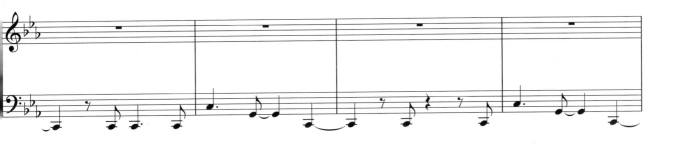

Cm7

I like the way you move. I like the way you move.

I love the way. ___ I love the way. ___

Rap Lyrics

Rap 1: Ready for action, nip it in the bud.
We never relaxin'. OutKast is everlastin'.
Not clashin', not at all.
But see, my nigga went up to do a little actin'.
Now that's for anyone askin'.
Give me one, pass 'em.
Drip, drip, drop, there goes an eargasm.
Now you comin' out the side of your face.
We tappin' right into your memory banks, thanks.
So click it or ticket, let's see your seatbelt fastened.
Trunk rattlin' like two midgets in the back seat wrestlin'
Speakerboxxx vibrate the tag.
Make it sound like aluminum cans in the bag.
But I know y'all wanted that eight-o-eight.
Can you feel that B-A-S-S, bass?
But I know y'all wanted that eight-o-eight.
Can you feel that B-A-S-S, bass?

Rap 2: The whole room fell silent. The girls all paused with glee.
Turnin' left, turnin' right, are they lookin' at me?
Well I was lookin' at them, there, there on the dance floor.
Now they got me in the middle feelin' like a man whore.
Especially the big girl. Big girls need love too.
No discrimination here, squirrel. So keep your hands off my cheeks.
Let me study how you ride the beat, you big freak.
Skinny slim women got the the camel-toe within' 'em.
You can hump them, lift them, bend them,
Give them something to remember.
Yell out "timber" when you fall through the chop shop.
Take a deep breath and exhale.
Your ex-male friend, boyfriend was boring as hell.
Well let me listen to the story you tell.
And we can make moves like a person in jail....
On the low, hoe!

WE ARE THE CHAMPIONS

Words and Music by
FREDDIE MERCURY

WE ARE THE WORLD

Words and Music by LIONEL RICHIE
and MICHAEL JACKSON

WEREWOLVES OF LONDON

Words and Music by WARREN ZEVON,
ROBERT WACHTEL and LeROY MARINEL

Moderate Rock

I saw a were-wolf with a Chi-nese men-u in his hand.

walk-ing through the streets of So - ho _____ in the rain.

He was look-ing for a place called Lee Ho _____ Fooks _____

1018

WHAT THE WORLD NEEDS NOW IS LOVE

Lyric by HAL DAVID
Music by BURT BACHARACH

With a Jazz Waltz feel

world needs now is love, sweet love.

It's the on-ly thing _____ that there's just _____ too lit-tle of. What the

WHEN I NEED YOU

Words by CAROLE BAYER SAGER
Music by ALBERT HAMMOND

Moderately, with feeling

WHEN I'M GONE

Words and Music by MATT ROBERTS,
BRAD ARNOLD, CHRISTOPHER HENDERSON
and ROBERT HARRELL

WHERE DO BROKEN HEARTS GO

Words and Music by CHUCK JACKSON
and FRANK WILDHORN

WOMAN

Words and Music by
JOHN LENNON

WHITE RABBIT

Words and Music b[...]
GRACE SLIC[...]

Moderately

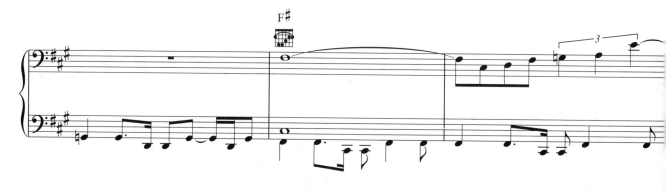

Psychedelic Stomp

WOO-HOO

Words and Music by
GEORGE DONALD McGRAW

YOU ARE NOT ALONE

Words and Music by
ROBERT KELLY

Verse 2:
You are not alone
I am here with you
Though you're far away
I am here to stay.
You are not alone
I am here with you
Though we're far apart
You're always in my heart.
But you are not alone.

Verse 3:
Just the other night
I thought I heard you cry
Asking me to go
And hold you in my arms.
I can hear your breaths
Your burdens I will bear
But first I need you here
Then forever can begin.

Verse 4:
You are not alone
I am here with you
Though you're far away
I am here to stay.
But you are not alone
I am here with you
Though we're far apart
You're always in my heart.
But you are not alone.

YOU BELONG TO ME

Words and Music by CARLY SIMON
and MICHAEL McDONALD

You Can't Hurry Love

Words and Music by EDWARD HOLLAND,
LAMONT DOZIER and BRIAN HOLLAND

YOU WERE MEANT FOR ME

Words and Music by JEWEL KILCHER
and STEVE POLTZ

I hear the clock. It's six A M.
I called my ma-ma, she was out for a walk. Con-
I brush my teeth. I put the cap back on.

I feel so far from where I've been.
soled a cup of cof-fee, but it did-n't want to talk. So, I
I know you hate it when I leave the light on. I

I got my eggs. I got my
picked up the pa-per, it was
pick up a cup and then I

YOU'RE IN MY HEART

Words and Music by
ROD STEWART

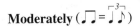

Moderately

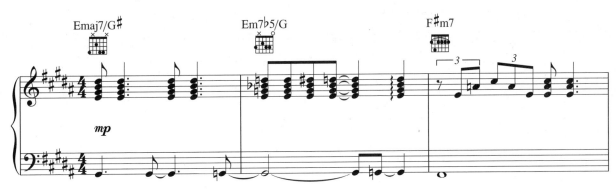

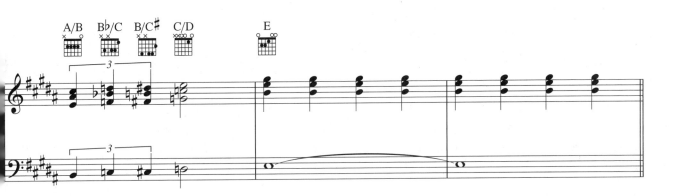

I did - n't know ___ what day it was ___ when you walked ___
I took all ___ those hab - its of yours that in the be -

YOU'VE GOT A FRIEND

Words and Music by
CAROLE KING

Vocal harmony sung 2nd time only

YOUR SONG

Words and Music by ELTON JOHN
and BERNIE TAUPIN

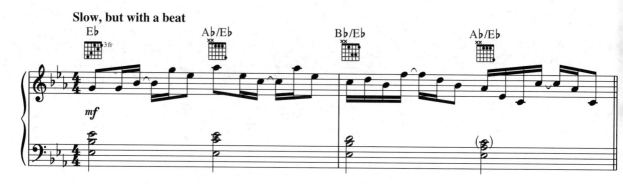

Slow, but with a beat

It's a lit - tle bit fun - ny, _____ this feel - ing in - side; _____
If I was a sculp - tor, _____ but then _ a - gain, no, _____ or a

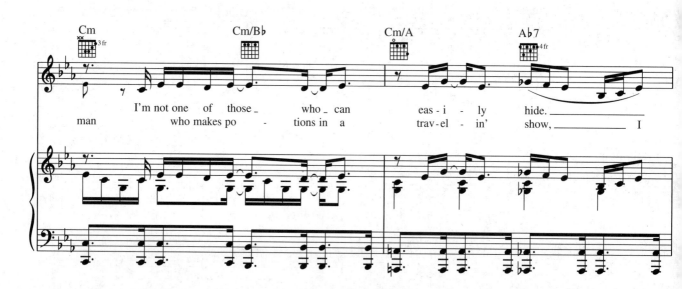

I'm not one of those _ who can eas - i - ly hide. _____
man who makes po - tions in a trav - el - in' show, _____ I

that I put down in words how won-der-ful life is while you're in the world.

you're in the world.

"YOU'VE LOST THAT LOVIN' FEELIN'"

Words and Music by BARRY MANN,
CYNTHIA WEIL and PHIL SPECTOR

et more BANG for your buck!

with budgetbooks

e value-priced collections feature **over 300 pages** of
o/vocal/guitar arrangements. With at least **70 hit**
s in most books for only $12.95, you pay **18 cents**
ss for each song!

Prices, contents & availability subject to change without notice.

FOR MORE INFORMATION,
SEE YOUR LOCAL MUSIC DEALER,
OR WRITE TO:

HAL•LEONARD®
CORPORATION
W. BLUEMOUND RD. P.O. BOX 13819
MILWAUKEE, WISCONSIN 53213

Visit Hal Leonard Online at
www.halleonard.com

BROADWAY SONGS

This jam-packed collection features 73 songs from 56 shows, including *Annie Get Your Gun, Beauty and the Beast, Cabaret, The Full Monty, Jekyll & Hyde, Les Misérables, The Music Man, Oklahoma!*, and more. Songs include: Any Dream Will Do • Cabaret • Consider Yourself • Footloose • Getting to Know You • I Dreamed a Dream • The Impossible Dream (The Quest) • Love Changes Everything • One • People • Summer Nights • The Surrey with the Fringe on Top • With One Look • You'll Never Walk Alone • and more.
00310832 P/V/G $12.95

CHILDREN'S SONGS

This fabulous collection includes over 100 songs that kids love, from favorite folksongs to movie theme songs, including: Alphabet Song • Be Our Guest • Bob the Builder "Intro Theme Song" • Do-Re-Mi • Eensy Weensy Spider • It's a Small World • London Bridge • My Favorite Things • Oh! Susanna • On Top of Spaghetti • Sesame Street Theme • SpongeBob SquarePants Theme Song • You've Got a Friend in Me • and more.
00311054 P/V/G $12.95

CHRISTMAS SONGS

100 holiday favorites, includes: All I Want for Christmas Is You • Away in a Manger • The Christmas Song (Chestnuts Roasting on an Open Fire) • Christmas Time Is Here • Feliz Navidad • The First Noel • Frosty the Snow Man • Grandma Got Run Over by a Reindeer • It's Beginning to Look Like Christmas • Let It Snow! Let It Snow! Let It Snow! • Merry Christmas, Darling • O Holy Night • Rockin' Around the Christmas Tree • Rudolph the Red-Nosed Reindeer • Silver Bells • What Child Is This? • Wonderful Christmastime • and more.
00310887 P/V/G $12.95

CLASSIC ROCK

A priceless collection of 70 of rock's best at a price that can't be beat! Includes: Ballroom Blitz • Bohemian Rhapsody • Come Sail Away • Don't Do Me Like That • Don't Stand So Close to Me • Eye in the Sky • Gloria • Owner of a Lonely Heart • Pink Houses • Rhiannon • Roxanne • Summer of '69 • Sweet Emotion • Walk of Life • Walk on the Wild Side • Wild Thing • You Really Got Me • and more.
00310906 P/V/G $12.95

CONTEMPORARY HITS

A cost-saving collection of 53 favorites, including: Amazed • Angel • Beautiful • Breathe • Clocks • Complicated • Don't Know Why • Drops of Jupiter (Tell Me) • Hanging by a Moment • Intuition • A Moment Like This • Smooth • Superman (It's Not Easy) • Underneath It All • and more.
00311053 P/V/G $12.95

COUNTRY SONGS

A great collection of 90 songs, including: Always on My Mind • Amazed • Boot Scootin' Boogie • Breathe • Cowboy Take Me Away • Down at the Twist and Shout • Elvira • Friends in Low Places • The Greatest Man I Never Knew • Hey, Good Lookin' • Lucille • Mammas Don't Let Your Babies Grow Up to Be Cowboys • Okie from Muskogee • Sixteen Tons • Walkin' After Midnight • You Are My Sunshine • and more.
00310833 P/V/G $12.95

EARLY ROCK

You can't go wrong with this collection of over 90 early rock classics, including: All Shook Up • At the Hop • Barbara Ann • Blue Suede Shoes • Bye Bye Love • Chantilly Lace • Crying • Duke of Earl • Fun, Fun, Fun • Great Balls of Fire • Hello Mary Lou • Hound Dog • In My Room • It's My Party • Jailhouse Rock • The Loco-Motion • Louie, Louie • Peggy Sue • Return to Sender • Rock Around the Clock • Shout • Splish Splash • Stand by Me • A Teenager in Love • Tequila • and more.
00311055 P/V/G $12.95

JAZZ STANDARDS

A collection of over 80 jazz classics. Includes: Alfie • Alright, Okay, You Win • Always in My Heart (Siempre En Mi Corazón) • Autumn in New York • Bewitched • Blue Skies • Body and Soul • Cherokee (Indian Love Song) • Do Nothin' Till You Hear from Me • Fever • Fly Me to the Moon (In Other Words) • Good Morning Heartache • Harlem Nocturne • I'll Be Seeing You • In the Mood • Isn't It Romantic? • Lazy Afternoon • Lover • Manhattan • Mona Lisa • Stella by Starlight • When Sunny Gets Blue • and more.
00310830 P/V/G $12.95

LATIN SONGS

An invaluable collection of over 80 Latin standards. Includes: Always in My Heart (Siempre En Mi Corazón) • Amor (Amor, Amor, Amor) • Bésame Mucho (Kiss Me Much) • Desafinado (Off Key) • Frenesí • The Girl from Ipanema (Garota De Ipanema) • How Insensitive (Insensatez) • La Bamba • Mambo #5 • Meditation (Meditacão) • Perfidia • Quizás, Quizás, Quizás (Perhaps, Perhaps, Perhaps) • Spanish Eyes • So Nice (Summer Samba) • and more.
00311056 P/V/G $12.95

LOVE SONGS

This collection of over 70 favorite love songs includes: And I Love Her • Crazy • Endless Love • Fields of Gold • I Just Called to Say I Love You • I'll Be There • Longer • (You Make Me Feel Like) A Natural Woman • Still • Wonderful Tonight • You Are So Beautiful • You Are the Sunshine of My Life • and more.
00310834 P/V/G $12.95

MOVIE SONGS

Over 70 memorable movie moments, including: Almost Paradise • Also Sprach Zarathustra, Opening Theme • Cole's Song • The Crying Game • Funny Girl • I Say a Little Prayer • Il Postino (The Postman) • Jailhouse Rock • Psycho (Prelude) • Puttin' On the Ritz • She • Southampton • Take My Breath Away (Love Theme) • Theme from "Terms of Endearment" • Up Where We Belong • The Way We Were • Where the Boys Are • and more.
00310831 P/V/G $12.95

POP/ROCK

This great collection of 75 top pop hits features: Adia • Angel • Back in the High Life Again • Barbara Ann • Crimson and Clover • Don't Cry Out Loud • Dust in the Wind • Hero • I Hope You Dance • If You're Gone • Jack and Diane • Lady Marmalade • Mony, Mony • Respect • Stand by Me • Tequila • Vision of Love • We Got the Beat • What's Going On • You Sang to Me • and more.
00310835 P/V/G $12.95

1003